INSIDER *Secrets* TO
SMALL BUSINESS SUCCE$$
More Money, More Freedom, More Fun

By Ann L. Carden

Business & Marketing Coach

DEDICATION

I would like to dedicate this book to my husband Clayton, my wonderful children Shane and Shaylyn and my amazing parents Donald and Marjorie.

Thank you for always being my support, believing in me and encouraging me to go after my dreams. I love each of you so much.

You, family, are my world!

Of course it is with a grateful heart that I give all the glory and praise to my Almighty God! God has always provided a path for me to work in what I love and to be able to work in ways that have made a difference in other's lives. God, you have always given me your consistent guidance, grace, mercy, strength and too many undeserved blessings to count. I know you have always been in control and I am so thankful.

John 15:5…I am the vine, you are the branches. If man remains in me and I in him, he will bear much fruit; apart from me you can do nothing.

To your success,

Ann L. Carden

CONTENTS

Acknowledgments

Forward

Introduction

1 Mindset For Success....................1

2 Passion Isn't Enough..................12

3 Marketing For Money..................24

4 Money Making Skills...................41

5 Make More Money Now...............45

6 Time is Money..........................49

ACKNOWLEDGMENTS

Thank you to the many mentors, coaches and business professionals that have inspired and taught me what you have learned. Thank you for sharing your gifts, talents and knowledge. Donna Krech (my first business coach), Dan Kennedy, Adrian Ulch, Brian Tracy and so many more.

Thank you to my husband, children, parents, friends, clients and many others in my path that have taught me, encouraged me and motivated me to strive to become more in life.

May God bless you all!

Foreword

In this book, Ann tackles some of the most basic fundamentals, principles and strategies she has learned in building and operating small business. Throughout this book's pages, she has woven her personal business experiences, mistakes, and pitfalls to give clarity to the reader, so they may avoid the same mistakes and implement the golden nougats that fill the pages.

The goal of this book is to help others in small business put fundamentals in place to build their business on a solid foundation. Without the basic fundamentals, it is very much like building a house on sand. The first big wave, or sign of stress, things start to cave in and crumble.

Apply what you learn in this book and start to build a strong foundation to accelerate your success in small business.

Through founding and building several successful businesses, Ann is now a Business and Marketing Coach, Trainer and Keynote Speaker, with a passion to share with others in small business the things she has learned.

Though there is nothing unique in this book on business fundamentals and principles, these are the very things every small business owner must know. By opening your mind to opportunities and implementing the things included in the pages, you are more likely to start running and operating your business in a less stressful and more profitable way.

It is important to remember that in business, you are responsible for everything that happens inside your business, good and bad. You can operate your business proactively - make more money and build the business of your dreams, or reactively - struggle, stress, stay broke and potentially fail

The choice is yours. The intention of this book is to set you on a course, to build your business so you will make **more money**, have **more freedom** and have **more fun** in your business and your life.

Today, more than ever before, there is more opportunity to create the success you want, break financial barriers and have financial freedom. In fact, it is more possible today than any other time in history. These are exciting times to be in small business or to be an entrepreneur with the technology available and thanks to the information age.

Introduction

After I left behind a corporate career to make a move with my family to a small town in the Midwest, I made the decision to stay home and raise my two small children. With my husband driving a long distance each day to his job, one vehicle and little opportunity to work outside the home, that decision left our family struggling financially.

The pivotal moment came when my four year old son needed new shoes and there was no money. As I sat and cried, I prayed to God for help and ideas to make extra money to help my family. I know God will always provide a way, when we turn to him and trust him. It was shortly thereafter that I started my first home-based business. Though I didn't know at the time, this taste for Entrepreneurship would be the course of my life for the years following.

Starting my first business in 1991, as a bootstrap entrepreneur, (someone with almost no money whom keeps investing back into the business until it becomes successful and profitable) I didn't have the luxury of a home computer, Google or the internet. This wonderful technology has changed the game in business.

The down side to this however, is that it is much easier for anyone and everyone to start a business. This has created its own set of problems. It has saturated the marketplace and created competition like no other time in history. It is inevitable and understandable that only the strong, knowledgeable, and best will survive.

To avoid falling into the 96% of all businesses that fail within the first five years, there are three critical things that you must consider doing to have the greatest chance of success...

1)Understand and implement business and marketing fundamentals.

2) **Build your business with diligence and speed so you are not left behind in the marketplace.**

3) **Invest in professional help to accelerate your business success.** This is a golden nougat! Not investing in a professional coach is by far the biggest mistake a small business owner can make. I made this very mistake and learned this for myself, the hard way.

Most in business don't know what they don't know. They think they can fly solo and figure things out on their own. It is what you don't know in business that is costing you the most.

When I look back at my biggest regret in business, it was not getting professional help long before I did. Hiring my first business coach was the one of the best decisions and investments I made in business. Even today, though I am a business and marketing coach, I never work without a coach or two of my own. Consider this…most millionaires work with coaches that are billionaires. What? Yes, they understand there is always more to learn for continued growth and success.

As business has changed through the years it becomes more and more evident there is no room for amateurs. Unless of course, you have unlimited funds and time.

Being exceptional at what you do is not enough to build a successful business. Most small business operators go into business with a dream of financial freedom. However, their lack of knowledge and understanding of business fundamentals unfortunately leaves them with nothing more than a low paying job.

Understand however, anyone can be successful in business. If I can do it, you can do it!

Success is actually predictable when you do the right things, in the right order, at the right time and of course…NEVER GIVE UP!

"There are no traffic jams on the extra mile ~ Zig Ziglar

CHAPTER 1
MINDSET

Decide On Success

You must have a success mindset. What do I mean by this? Well, first you have to make the decision that you want success.

For many years growing businesses, I never really thought, "I want success." Don't misunderstand, I knew I wanted my businesses to grow, but I didn't have a "success mindset." In fact it was just the opposite. The mindset I had was not to fail. They are not at all the same thing.

To have a success mindset, you have to make the conscious decision that you want to succeed. Then, start putting a plan in place to achieve it. Start to think and do what other very successful people do. Study them, watch them and learn from them. Don't reinvent the wheel. There is nothing you will go through in business that others have not already gone through. The key is to learn from them.

Scarcity or Abundance

There are two types of mindsets about money. A mindset of scarcity and a mindset of abundance. One will help you strive to make your financial dreams come true, while the other will put limits on your success and financial freedom.

When I was building my first health club, I had a scarcity mindset. I didn't know it at the time, but now as I look back, I can't help but cringe at my scarcity way of thinking.

There were approximately 15,000 people in the town where my health club was located. Statistics showed that in the fitness industry, roughly about 10% of the population actually had a health club membership. My way of thinking, limited my success as I took those numbers to heart.

That meant only 1500 people would actually go to a health club . Since there were three in our town, the 1500 people would be divided between the three. This meant, my business would get about 500 of those people. Subconsciously, that held me back. That is a scarcity way of thinking. How ridiculous to even think that way.

Understand that as a business owner, you have control over your business. Being more knowledgeable in business and marketing fundamentals, those statistics have no relevance to achieving higher success. Don't allow yourself to put limits on what can be achieved.

Let's look at that same situation with an

abundance mindset: There are 15,000 people in the town. The question is, what can be done to get as many as possible to join my club? When they join my club, what other packages, programs and products can be offered for them to purchase? By insuring that there will be many other things available to help them reach their goals will also insure additional revenue is generated. The revenue that could be made would have no limits! Do you see the difference in a scarcity and an abundance mindset?

Which mindset do you have?

Money Guilt

Another thing to consider in regards to a scarcity mindset is guilt about making money. This is common with business owners that have a business that helps people. As a coach, I see this over and over again. Business owners say, they don't really care about making money, they love helping people. Well, if that's true, then why not just offer your services and products for free and become a charity? The purpose of business is to make money! If you don't make money, you won't stay in business. This will certainly limit the people you can help.

Maybe great wealth is not something you desire. However, these are two very different things.

We all need money. It is a necessity, but it is also a tool that can make a tremendous difference in your life or the lives of others. Therefore, I want to challenge you to shift your thinking. Is it not true that the more money you make, the more of a difference you can make, and the more people you can help? Is it not true that when money is not a concern, you can seize new opportunities in life that you may otherwise not be able to take advantage of?

Looking back, I can remember times when I felt guilt that my business was doing extremely well and the money was good. I was careful to not let others know. I can remember one time purchasing a much needed new car. When my employees or members of my club asked me about it, I felt guilt and embarrassment, feeling as if I had done something wrong. However, that couldn't have been further from the truth. The endless hours worked, time from my family, 24/7 stress, never getting away from my business, going without pay many times while my employees never did and the risk involved in having a business, were all the reasons why that guilt and way of thinking was and is ridiculous.

When you work extremely hard for the money made and you are blessed for that work, there should be no guilt. If this is how you think, or maybe why you are not reaching your true potential, please choose to think differently. It will always hold you back from your dreams and from being all God is calling you to be. If you are in God's will, he wants abundance for you. Be grateful for his blessings.

If you have a guilt or a scarcity way of

thinking about money, challenge yourself to start thinking differently and see how it will start to change your financial future.

Learn to Earn

So, how do you get a success mindset? Become a lifelong student! Successful people really understand this. They never stop learning! They know and understand that the more you learn, the more you will earn. Learning, growing and personal development should be built into your daily schedule each and every day. Think of it as your training to continue to do business. Applying this principal and habit to my life every day, continues to add ideas, growth and opportunities I never thought possible.

Most people will resist this idea saying they don't have the time. An easy way to start doing this, is to go to auto mobile university (a Zig Ziglar concept.) This means that every time you are in your car, listen to an audio training program or audio books that will teach you things, motivate you, inspire you and help you to personally grow.

Doing the math at one time, I discovered that, without actually realizing it, I had completed what was equivalent to one and a half years of college just by learning every time I was in my car and driving back and forth to work for a year. It was this very thing that inspired me to put out my very first audio program…BASIC BUSINESS BOOTCAMP for business owners and entrepreneurs. This can be purchased @ www.anncardencoaching.com

Today this is one of the most valuable and important habits I have. Through a variety of coaches, mentors, business seminars, business and marketing books and training programs, business became easier and I found myself working smarter instead of harder. Yes, this one habit alone has fast tracked my business success, made me more money with much less stress and given me new opportunities.

It has never been easier to become a student

and to learn new things. You no longer have to head out to a library to grab a book. We have so much available to learn from and gain new knowledge with the click of a mouse.

When you consistently learn and grow, it will not be a question of when, but a question of where your next great idea, opportunity or new thought will come from. Your real money making or million dollar idea could come from a book, a training program, a video or a coach.

Statistics show, most people don't even read a book after they get out of high school. Statistics also show that your income is usually a direct reflection of your knowledge. What do you do every day to continue to learn and grow?

Consider this, successful people are willing to invest time doing things that most people will not do.

Understand however, learning isn't enough.

Having knowledge without application or implementation is useless! Implementation and accountability of the things learned, is one of the great values of having a professional coach.

"You are where you choose to be."
~Jim Rohn

CHAPTER 2
PASSION ISN'T ENOUGH!

To get what you want and have predictable success, you must understand the basic fundamentals of business and marketing. You must hone your business skills. 80% of all small business owners and entrepreneurs never see the success that they could have, or reach their full potential. Why? Many people start a business because of a passion or with a skill where they are excellent. Once they have invested their time and money, they quickly realize running and growing a business is not as easy as they imagined.

It happens more often than not and is the reason why so many businesses fail. You don't have to have a business degree to start a business, but that doesn't mean you know what to do once you get started. Business skills and fundamentals are vital to the success one will see. Because most don't have years and unlimited money to make their business profitable, professional help (such as a coach) can be one of the best investments you can make. The right coach will not only help you see success faster, they will also keep you from wasting valuable time and money.

It is not enough to be great at what you do. This does not and most likely will not guarantee business success or profits.

For many years, I wanted to become great in fitness and nutrition. I loved it and couldn't have been more passionate. I attended various trainings and seminars to learn as much as I possibly could about fitness and nutrition. It was important to become great in my industry. However, there came a time that it was not growing my business any longer. I kept working harder and harder. Became exhausted and burnt out and still was not making the money I wanted to make. There had to be a better way.

Business Made Simple

I made the decision to start becoming a student of business. Instead of fitness and nutrition books, I started lining my book shelves with business books. I became dedicated to working with coaches and mentors. I invested in training programs and attended business seminars.

Learning how to be better in business taught me how to stop trading time for dollars and how to put basic fundamentals and systems in place. Not only did this allow exponential growth, but it gave me more time back in my life and more income. Business is actually very simple. Not easy, but simple, when you really understand business.

One of the first fundamentals of business is setting goals. Know what you want and then put a plan in place to achieve it. What is your vision for your business? Do you want a job?

Do you want multiple locations? Do you want to build a franchise you can sell to other's? Decide what you want. Start with the end in mind and then work backwards to put a plan in place to reach your destination.

It is important to write your goals down! Put them in a place where you can see them frequently. Refer to them often to stay on track with your plan.

Setting goals will be the first step in building a strong foundation for your business. It will allow you to see your strengths and needs for the business. It will also help you see any gaps you may have in your skills and knowledge that could potentially hold you back.

Science has proven that just setting a goal will tell your brain to start moving toward that goal. It has been proven that there is a real, physical, subconscious response, that goes on in the brain when we set goals. Your brain will automatically look for ways to achieve the goal. Our mind is powerful and quite amazing!

S.M.A.R.T. Goals

One great way to set goals is to set up S.M.A.R.T. goals. This is an acronym for specific, measurable, attainable, realistic and time-bound or timely.

Specific

Who, what, where, when, which, and why. Remember, you can't hit a target you can't see. Answer these questions.

1) Who will be involved?
2) What do I want to accomplish?
3) Where will this be or where will I do this?
4) When will I accomplish this?
5) Which are the strengths that I should build on. Which are my weaknesses and gaps that may be a factor in limiting my success.
6) Why do I really want what I want? A powerful why will keep the fire going when things get hard. If the why is not powerful enough, you will lack the drive, enthusiasm and energy to push through the rough spots.

Measurable

You must be able to know how you are doing towards your goal.

When you measure your progress, you stay on track, reach your target dates, and experience the excitement of achievement that will motivate you to continue on.

Establish solid criteria for measuring progress toward the attainment of your goal.

To determine if your goal is measurable, ask questions such as, how much, how many and how will I know when it is accomplished?

Let's think about it in terms of someone that wants to lose weight. How much do they want to lose? Do they want to get to a certain weight or size? Imagine having no real goal except that you want to lose weight. How likely will it be that you will stay motivated. How will you ever know when you get there?

This is also true in business. Having a

measurable goal will allow you to see where you are and how much further you have to go.

Attainable

When you identify goals that are most important to you, you can now begin to figure out how to reach them. You will start to develop the attitudes, abilities, skills, and financial capacity to reach them. You start to see opportunities and develop new ideas you maybe didn't see before that may help you reach your goal.

You can attain most any goal you set when you plan your steps wisely and are willing to do what it will take to reach them.

Realistic

To be realistic, a goal must represent an objective which you are willing and able to work for. You can simultaneously set a goal that is high, but can still be realistic. Many times these types of goals will help you stretch and grow in skills and knowledge.

Sometimes a high goal is easier to reach because it requires higher motivation. Some of the hardest things accomplished in life many times seem easier, as you loved what you were doing.

Time-bound

It is believed that the Time-bound aspect in a S.M.A.R.T goal is as important as setting the goal itself. Having a time limit or time-frame for a goal can be a great motivator to keep you on task.

By nature, we are procrastinators. However, in our society and especially in the work place or business, we are driven by time, by an internal and external clock. We respond and live by time. We never seem to have enough of it and it is our most valuable asset. One thing is for sure, we will never get more time back and we cannot manufacture it.

Making time count and managing time well is

something highly successful people do well; many times in minutes. Therefore, it only stands to reason, that to achieve something, we need to have a sense of urgency to accomplish it within a time-frame. Working within a time frame allows us to measure the results and potential outcome. It can often allow us to draw from an extra energy, strength or motivation from within ourselves to meet the deadline or not fail.

What Now?

Once you have the goal, you can put the plan in place to reach it. It won't magically happen on its own.

Consider this; if you were going to build a beautiful home, you would never just hire workers, buy all the materials and not give the workers any kind of a plan or blueprint, right? Would you send the workers in and tell them to just start hammering together some wood with some nails and build your beautiful home? Of course you wouldn't. Who knows what you would get.

The same is true in a business. To build a successful and sustainable business, there must be a plan or blueprint on how that will happen.

I am not referring to an eighty page business plan that you will never look at. The best plan for a small business is a strategic, step by step plan. This can be accomplished by breaking the goal into bite size chunks by year, quarters, months, weeks and days. It sounds difficult to do, but breaking goals down into smaller steps makes it much simpler to stay focused and achieve the desired results.

Leaving Things to Chance

If there's one thing that's certain when you start or build a business it's that, if you don't set up a goal, and you don't design a plan to reach that goal, you are leaving your business to chance.

It is taking on an attitude in your business of 'whatever will be will be.' Most small business owners and entrepreneurs are guilty of running their business without any goal or plan. The result is usually that they will never reach full potential, will have more stress than necessary, and most often waste money and time.

Take Action

Now that you clearly know what you want to achieve, and you have a plan in place, the next step is to work the plan. Be an "Action Taker." It's not just going to work itself, right? You have to put one foot in front of the other every single day, and you have to do the work.

A goal, plan and action will allow you to work with direction and focus. It will allow you to measure progress and be proactive instead of reactive in your business. It will help you be more productive and work on the things that matter most in your business.

In a small business, you wear many hats and it's extremely easy to get lost in the everyday clutter. You may find your valuable time being spent putting out fires in your business or busy work. Before you realize it, you have spent endless hours on activity, instead of the productive things that grow the business and the profits. However, when you have a clear goal and a plan in place, it becomes like your GPS to reach your destination. This alone will ensure more success and enjoyment as a business owner.

CHAPTER 3
MARKETING FOR MONEY

You can achieve predictable growth and success if you master strategic marketing. In the next few chapters, I will go into more detail about strategic marketing. However, it is important to first understand exactly what it is and what it can mean to your business.

In today's marketplace, competition is higher than ever before. Every business out there is fighting to be noticed. The average person is bombarded with thousands of marketing messages a day. How do you get your business above all that noise to be noticed by potential prospects? If you don't know how to strategically market your business in the right way, you probably won't.

Strategic marketing is all about the right message, to the right people and in the right way. What you say and how you say it are the most important things. Then a plan can be put in place of where you will say it.

You are really in the marketing business!

Understand that marketing should be a top priority in your business and must be done consistently. If no one knows about you or they forget about you, it doesn't matter how great you are at what you do. Don't sit and wait for things to happen. Just because a business opens their doors, hangs a sign and maybe runs a print ad or two, doesn't mean people are going to flood through their doors. That's simply not the case for most. Even if that happens with a new business, they must continue to market to stay in front of those customers, so they are driving sales and are not forgotten.

Most business owners don't have a strategic marketing plan. If they market, it is usually tactical with no real plan. Most marketing dollars spent are most often a huge cost to their business, with little or no return on their money. Running a print ad or sending out a direct mail piece when one needs customers or money are all tactics.

For several years in business, I made these same mistakes. Not understanding and mastering world class marketing fundamentals, will cost you more wasted money than you can even imagine.

Don't Buy The Lie

Through the years after almost failing in one of my businesses, I went on a personal mission to learn and understand marketing for small business. I searched for the best in the world for my education. It has been and still is one of the most valuable things I invested time and money in to learn.

As a coach, most likely the first thing I help others implement in their business is a marketing strategy to generate more leads.

Knowing how to do this effectively and strategically will save years of wasted money.

For most in small business, marketing is one of the highest expenses they have. It consistently sucks money from their business and most often offers nothing in return. However, most figure out quickly that their business is dead in the water without it. Learning the secrets of small business marketing and implementing a strategic marketing plan, will insure your marketing is an investment rather than a cost. When done in the right way, your marketing can be predictable, trackable and have a highly profitable return.

One of the biggest lies people will tell you about small business is the concept of *branding*. It is most often this very concept that can cause a small business to go broke and even fail. Don't buy into the lie you are probably being told by every advertising rep and so called marketing company out there. The lie that you must brand your business and run awareness advertising to build your brand.

WRONG! Everything you have been taught about marketing this way is wrong. You do not have the money or the resources to brand your small business with awareness marketing.

I am not referring to the design on your website, brochures, logo, business cards, etc. That is something very different. I am referring to advertising and marketing your business to generate leads.

Back in the early days of advertising (1800's and 1900's), advertising was the way it should be done now. Ads would show how and why they were better than their competitors. They educated prospective buyers on why they should buy from them.

Once television was commercially introduced for the first time in 1945, it changed everything. Up until that time, advertising was limited to radio, print advertising in a few magazines and newspapers and maybe the Sears catalog. But, with television commercials, advertisers could reach almost everyone in the country for a few thousand dollars a minute. However, there were also only three channels, so with the demand, prices shot sky high. To meet the demand, commercials went from one or two minutes, to thirty seconds. This meant that advertisers had less time to educate us and build a case as to why we should buy from them. As a result, they started using slogans.

The use of slogans made it harder for people to be educated and convinced to make a buying decision. So, big companies started using the C & R approach. C for creativity and R for repetition. If they ran a commercial that was crazy, weird, funny, unusual, shocking and spent millions of dollars, running it millions of times, their brand and slogan stuck in consumers heads and they remembered it, whether they wanted to or not. Then, when they had a need for the product or service, they could remember the brand.

That was the start of the Brand-builder era. Ad agencies used the brand-building formula for all of its clients, even the small businesses without much money. Business schools started teaching brand marketing and the graduates learned only one way to market. After a while, no one even questioned this kind of marketing.

We have become conditioned to believe that this is the way to market your small business and it the very thing that will cause wasted money and no return.

I am going to repeat again the very thing I said at the beginning of this chapter…you do not have the money or the time to brand your small business with awareness marketing!

Have you ever heard an advertising rep that is trying to sell you an ad contract to their paper or magazine tell you, that people need to see your business ad several times to build your brand?

I wish I had back all the money I wasted buying into that lie. Now, in all fairness, it is not their fault. They don't know any different. But, the next time you hear someone say that to you, run! The truth is, if you do not get response from an advertisement the very first time you run it, fix the ad. Running it for weeks on end will only continue to cost you money.

Big Warning!

A big mistake many business owners make, is spending money to hire a marketing company to market their business. This is a really bad idea, if you don't understand fundamentals of strategic marketing. In most cases, they don't know how to market your business any better than you do. If you don't become great at marketing your business first to know what works, you are going to throw your money away. However, once you have mastered strategic marketing for your business, you can then outsource the tasks or technical work to a marketing company.

Following The Leader

The second most common mistake that most make is trying to market like everyone else in their industry. Their marketing may not be working for them, so why would you want to copy it? If you don't understand great marketing, you may just be copying other's mistakes.

Years ago, when I didn't really understand how to effectively market, I would run a newspaper print ad for my health club. A week later, my competitors would copy and run the same ad and the same offer. It was as if they would replace my logo with theirs and run the ad. It used to really frustrate me. However, back then, I didn't understand why my marketing never worked for my business. I bet they wondered why their marketing was not working. Since they were copying mine, and I was getting little to no return, I am sure they experienced the same results, right? The only one to profit was the newspaper. Don't follow the leader unless it is clear the leader really knows what they are doing.

Learning for yourself how to effectively and strategically market your business, will help bring you consistent and qualified business over and over again at will.

It will also allow you to quit competing on price, dominate your market, and crush your competition. With the right message and having a clear understanding of your target market, you can now market to your target audience with less money and effort. It can even help you be able to generate as many leads as your business can handle.

At the time I am writing this book, I am still the owner of a fitness club for women. I have over twenty eight competitors within a two mile radius of my fitness club. Because I understand how to effectively market that business, it continues to grow and succeed. With my professional help or my training programs, I can show you exactly how to do this for your small business.

Choose Your Target Market

A target market is simply the group of customers or clients who will purchase a specific product or service. This group of people all have something in common, often age, gender, hobbies, or location.

Your particular target market, then, are the people who will buy your offering. This includes both existing and potential customers, all of whom are motivated to do one of three things:

- Fulfill a need
- Solve a problem
- Satisfy a desire

Since competition today is higher than it has ever been in small business, it's the number one key to building your business. To build, maintain, and grow your business, you need to know who your customers are, what they do, what they like, and why they would buy your product or service. Getting this wrong – or not taking the time to get it right – will cost you time, money, and potentially the success of your business.

The Importance of Knowing Your Target Market

Knowledge and understanding of your target

market is the key to the success of your business. Without it, your product or service positioning, pricing, marketing strategy, and eventually your business, could very quickly fall apart.

If you don't intimately know your target market, you run the risk of making mistakes when it comes to establishing pricing, product mix, or service packages. You will waste marketing dollars chasing prospects that will not be your customers. Your marketing strategy will lack direction, and produce minimal results at best.

Even if your marketing message and unique selling proposition (USP) are clear, it means nothing unless it reaches the right people.

Benefits Not Features

Market your business with benefits instead of features. This means you must put yourself in your customer's shoes and insure your marketing shows the benefits they will get from buying whatever it is you are selling.

How you are going to help them? It is not about what you have and who you are. Your marketing must be all about what you can do for them.

The most common mistake made in marketing today is using what we call jargon. Jargon is all about how great you are, what makes you better, why they should buy from you and how many years you have been in business. Don't be offended when I say, no one cares! It isn't about you. The customer wants to know what *they* will get from doing business with you. Convince them they want or need what you have and why. It's that simple.

Before I understood the right way to market, I would run ads that would say, we are a 16,000 square foot health club. We have 150 pieces of equipment. We have an indoor track. We have a spa, sauna, smoothie bar, daycare, full weight loss center, and so on. Then, I would get frustrated because people wouldn't respond to those ads and my money would be wasted. Why would they respond? Nowhere in any of those ads was it about what they would want and how we could help them get what they want. Nowhere in my marketing was it about them.

There was nothing that hit their hot buttons. Nothing that told them how we could improve their health to get off medications, help them lose two sizes in thirty days, look great in their clothes again, or move and feel like they are ten years younger. The marketing I did was never about those things. What would make them want to do business with me? Most people in small business today are making the same mistakes.

Pull up three or four websites in the same industry and it is likely they will all look the same. They most likely even say the same things about why you should buy from them. If you remove the name of the company, you probably wouldn't even be able to tell the difference in the companies. They all use jargon and say the same things about why you should buy from them.
To understand what I'm trying you show you,

put yourself in the customer shoes and then think about what you have in your business. How can you craft your marketing to use hot buttons in your headline to capture their attention?

Example Headline:
Are You Sick and Tired of the Muffin Top Hanging Over the Top of Your Jeans?

Sub-Headline:
Get rid of your muffin top in our 21 day belly fat burner program.

Now give them a list of what they will get and the benefits from each of those features.

Make A Great Offer

Make an offer in your advertising that is compelling and hard to pass up. A low risk, or low barrier offer works best. Make your offer something that is easy for them to say yes! This doesn't always need to be price driven. It can offer a huge value, a special bonus, or a no risk guarantee.

Call-To-Action

Make sure every ad you ever run has a call-to-action. This is about telling them specifically what to do next such as, 'Call us at …' or 'Go to our website and get it now' or 'Bring this offer into our store to receive…'

Contact Information

Put your business name, logo and contact information towards the bottom of your advertisements and marketing instead of the top, as most do. Use the prime real estate, across the top to grab their attention and a sub-headline to keep them engaged. The body of the ad is to offer more information to educate and compel the prospect further to be interested. The bottom should have the offer with a call to action, the guarantee you make them and your contact information. Once your potential clients want what you offer, they will look for your information to contact you. Remember that your marketing is not about you, who you are and what you do. No one cares about your beautiful logo, but you.

"He who markets the best, WINS!"
~ Ann Carden

CHAPTER 4
MONEY MAKING SKILLS

Master your communication skills. Your communication skills are your money making skills. Your communication skills are the skills that will make you great on the phone, great at networking, great at booking appointments, great at customer service, and great at converting and closing sales. Master these skills and you will never be unemployed! You'll always have the option to work. You'll always be able to make money. Again, these are your money making skills! Master these skills and you will have them for life.

Sales and communication is not about talent as people think. These are skills that can be learned by anyone.

One of my coaching clients was generating a lot of leads through her website. However, when she followed up on those leads, she wasn't getting an appointment with them. We worked on her phone skills, put a phone script in place and fixed the problem. She no longer had trouble getting appointments. We then discovered that she was struggling to close the sale and convert them into paying clients. I worked with her on her closing techniques, and two hours later, she called back a prospect that had not previously hired her and closed her into an agreement for over $2200. Proof that they are just skills that can be learned.

Being in my own businesses for years, it has been more the norm than not for people to tell me they aren't good in sales and they don't like sales. In business, it is going to be a much harder road if you lack in this area. Even if you hire sales people, someone needs to train them on how to turn prospects into clients or customers. This is just my particular way of thinking, but I have always felt the need and desire to master anything I was going to expect others to do in my business. I want to know how to do things first, so I can adequately train someone else to do the tasks. The exception of course would be more professional services that would be contracted out such as; accounting work, website, graphic design, etc.

It's my opinion, and the opinion of many business experts, that small business owners need to become good at communication and skills, even if you don't like it. It will be a part of a strong foundation to build your business. It will allow and open more opportunities and doors for success.

Understand, no one is born a salesperson. You are not birthed as a salesperson. Have you ever known a baby salesperson? Of course not. People have to learn these skills.

There was a woman that worked for me for

eight years in my fitness business. She was an excellent employee and had many wonderful qualities. When the needs for my business changed, I informed my staff they would be required to help sell and would have sales goals. This woman cried! She said "I'm not a sales person, I don't want to sell. I'm not good at sales."

Long story short…she stuck with me, trained hard, worked at it, and became the top producer. She became great at sales. I don't know if she ever really liked it, or even if it ever really got comfortable for her, but they were skills that she learned. Today, she owns her own personal training business. I couldn't be more proud of her.

Building your communication and sales skills may push you out of your comfort zone, but master them anyway. The best things happen outside of our comfort zone.

CHAPTER 5
MAKE MORE MONEY NOW

Out of the Box Thinking

To increase revenue and profits in your business, become a great innovator. A common mistake for small business owners is the idea that they need to continue spending money to make more money. Business owners are constantly buying and adding new products and services without thinking of ways to generate cash flow and profits without spending more. As you do need to consistently add income streams and new ways to increase revenue and cash flow, I want to challenge you to be more innovative and creative. Look for ways to make money without increasing costs. I like to call this "Out Of The Box Thinking."

Ways to achieve this include:

- Joint Ventures
- Bundling products and services (adding value without additional cost, then pricing the entire bundle)
- Create new packages, services or programs with what you already have in your business. Think of ways to put a new spin on something old and run it as a new promotion or a sale. Get creative!
- Up-sell and cross-sell strategies (can add as much as 35% or more in additional revenue.) McDonald's has been using this strategy for years. Would you like fries with that? Would you like to supersize for just $1 more? Sure!
- Add value in some way (with little or no cost to you) and get a higher price.

- Organize a referral program for existing customers
- Think of different ways to increase the number of transactions with your existing customers. For example, let's say you already have 100 customers and you find a way to sell just $25 more a month to those customers. You will be adding $30,000 to your business revenue just by selling to your existing clientele!

If you're looking to make more money immediately, create a new package or service. Now, market that idea to people that already know, like and trust you, or people that you have their contact information. Market your innovative idea to people in the exact order below. This will insure the most revenue and profits with little to no marketing money to be spent.

- First, market the new program or service to people whom already do business with you
- Second, market it to people who have

done business with you in the past
- Third, to people who have previously thought of doing business with you
- Fourth, everyone else

Pick up the phone, email them, reach out to them on social media, send them an invitation or a sales letter. Marketing to people who you already have contact with is an easy way to generate immediate cash flow.

Internal marketing is often overlooked in business. Business owners are always trying to generate new leads and, many times, leave a lot of money on the table by not tapping this resource.

In marketing, these people are referred to as low hanging fruit. These are the people right in front of you and ripe for the picking. Go market to them first. This strategy alone can put money in your pocket today or tomorrow. This is very much like generating revenue from thin air. Don't miss out on this money for your business!!

CHAPTER 6
TIME IS MONEY

Why did you get into business for yourself?
Was it to be your own boss? Choose your
own hours? Have more time with the family?
Spend more time doing what you love?
Chances are, you answered yes to all of these
questions.

These days, you probably wonder where the
time went. Why you spent 12 hours at work
and barely made a dent in your to-do list. We
already know that time is a key resource for
you and your business, but it's also a key
resource in your life. Harnessing and
leveraging time is the only way to enjoy life,
and have a profitable business at the same
time.

What most business owners don't realize is that time – and the time of all employees – requires the same attention and diligent management.

Time will never manage itself. The decision to make a pro-active effort to manage your time must come from you. Once you have committed to taking ownership for your own time management, there are a host of tools available to you. First, understand how much your time is actually worth, and where you are currently spending it.

What is Your Time Worth?

Ever wonder what your time is actually worth?

Here's a quick way to figure it out:
A. Target annual income
B. Working days in a year = 235
C. Working hours in a day = 7
D. Working hours in a year = 1,645
A divided by D = YOUR HOURLY

WORTH (before tax + expenses)

This is a very simple calculation intended to put your time in perspective. In reality, no one is productive for each of the 1,645 hours. Various studies have put actual productivity at anywhere between 25 minutes and four hours per day. Either way, there's a lot of room for improvement.

Let's look at it another way:

A. Your age = ___
B. Days in a year = 365
C. Days spent on earth to date = (A x B)
D. Average life expectancy = 70
E. Total projected days on earth = (D x B)
F. Estimated days left = (E – C)

This exercise isn't intended to scare you, but bring your attention to the importance of choosing how you spend each hour you have available. It's a choice! By developing the skills required to manage your time, you will not only have a profitable business, but a rewarding and balanced life.

Time Theft

Chances are – if you're like most people – you have no idea where your time goes. You're likely frustrated by the fact that you can spend 10, 12, even 14 hours a day working, and not make a dent in your to-do list, or only bill half of those hours.

When we're too busy and overloaded with work, we often switch into reactive mode. We can't make it to the bottom of the pile, and end up handling issues and making decisions at the last minute. One of the great benefits of choosing to become proactive in time management is that you can become proactive in all other areas of your business. When in proactive mode, you can take steps to grow your business through networking, building programs, and establishing systems.

Before you investigate where your time goes, let's take a look at the top five culprits of modern-day time theft:

1. Your Email

How many times a day do you check your email? Is Outlook or Mail constantly running on your desktop? Email – internal, external, personal and business – clogs up your day like no other communication channel. For many of us, it's possible to spend the entire day writing and responding to emails without even glancing at our inbox. The number of emails sent and received each day by the average person is 147. Multiply that by an average of two minutes per message, and you have spent almost five hours on email in a single day.

2. Your Cell Phone

Cell phones have created convenience, security, and the luxury of telecommuting. Cell phones have also created a society that expects to be able to reach you at any moment, or at least receive instant responses to their calls. Your cell phone not only robs you of your time during the day, but also during the evenings and on weekends when you are not at work.

3. Your Open-Door Policy

If you make it easy for your staff and associates to interrupt you, they will. Too often, open-door policies are set up by human resource departments to create clear communication channels. Instead, they create a clog of employees lined up at your door seeking immediate answers to non-emergent issues.

4. Meetings

How many times have you been to a meeting that was scheduled to be an hour, and ended up lasting three? How often do you attend unnecessary meetings? This is common in networkers. Are you getting value from the meetings, or are you having fun and being social? Are you attending meetings that consistently run off-topic? Meetings can be a huge source of wasted time – your valuable time. In an ownership position, your day may consist of back-to-back meetings, leaving only your evening hours to complete the tasks that should have been done during the day.

5. YOU!

Every person has daily habits that sabotage

their ability to work productively and efficiently. Many entrepreneurs and business owners can't separate business hours from leisure hours. Some get caught in a time warp while surfing the internet. Others - mainly overachievers – can become paralyzed by perfectionism or procrastination. Mainly, we just don't have the tools to schedule and structure our time in a way that fits with our working style.

Where Does Your Time Go?

So far we've seen that time is a resource that should be as carefully managed as cash, we've figured out what your time is worth, and looked at the top five culprits of time theft. You've committed to taking steps to become a better time manager. What now?

Personal Time Management Research Exercise

The next step is to take a good and *honest* look at how you spend your time. Once you understand your patterns and habits, you begin to implement the strategies in this chapter that will make you a better time manager.

Step 1: Time Audit
Be honest, and be specific. Include time spent in transit, surfing the web, interacting with clients and colleagues, as well as how your time is spent at home in the evenings. The more information you can record, the easier it will be to analyze your time management skills in step two.

Step 2: Time Categorization
Record your time for three days. Once you have recorded your time for three days, sit down with all three sheets in front of you and identify the following using different colored markers or highlighters:

- Driving, public transportation or other travel
- Eating, including food preparation
- Personal errands
- Exercise
- Watching TV

- Sleeping, including naps
- Using the computer, personal use only
- Being with family / friends
- Emailing, including checking, reading, and returning messages
- Talking on the phone, including checking and returning messages
- Internal meetings
- External meetings
- Administrative work
- Client work
- Non-client, non-administrative work

Step 3: Time Analysis

Now that you have identified how you have spent your time, go through one more time and identify if you have spent enough, too much, or too little time on each main task.

Then, based on your observations, answer the following questions:

1. What patterns do you notice about how you spend your time during the day? (i.e., When are you most productive? Least productive? Most or least interrupted?)

2. Write down the four highest priorities in your life right now. Does your timesheet reflect these priorities?
3. If you have more time, what would you do?
4. If you had less time, what wouldn't you do?
5. Could you remove the items in question four and add the items in question three? Why or why not?
6. Is procrastination a problem for you? How much?

Profitable Time Management

There are many ways to curb time theft and refine your time management ability. Through a solid understanding of how you currently spend – and waste – time, you can determine which strategies you need to implement to correct unproductive behavior.

For many years in my fitness business I instructed classes, trained clients and made smoothies at the smoothie bar. That did not help my business to grow. As I was spending endless hours a day on these tasks producing around $50-$75 an hour, I should have been spending my time producing thousands of dollars an hour for my business, which was the annual value of a training or weight loss client. Do the math yourself. Not a very smart way to run business.

Here are several ways you can turn less of your time into more money:

1. Set Clear Priorities

The foundation of time management is a clear understanding of what your time is best spent on. Once you accept that you can't do everything, you need to decide what needs to be completed now, what can be completed later, and what someone else can complete. Each to-do list you create should be put through this filter, and reorganized so the highest priority items are on top, and the lowest priority items are less visible, or on the bottom.

Once you have established your priorities – which will also naturally reflect the priorities and goals of your business – stick to them.

Just because someone else feels something is of a high priority doesn't mean it holds the same status next to your other tasks.

Prioritization is also helpful in your personal life and leisure time. Your spare time is precious – so make sure you are clear on how you would like to spend it.

2. Use Your Skills – Delegate Your Weaknesses

As a business owner, your day naturally consists of tasks you dislike performing. Some are essential – signing checks, reviewing financial statements, and other business maintenance – while others are simply not within your skill set.

If you are a strong public speaker, but struggle with report writing – delegate to a copywriter or editor. If you own a retail store and have no experience in design – outsource your signage. These freelance professionals often cost half as much as you, and take half as long to complete the task. Your time is saved for tasks that use and strengthen your skills effectively, your stress is managed, and ultimately a better product is produced.

3. Delegate, Delegate, Delegate

As a small business owner, the only way you will ever get everything done is by delegating. Delegation is a vital skill that needs to be refined and practiced, and once mastered is the key to profitable time management.

Too often, owners and managers believe that it will be faster or more efficient to complete the task themselves than to train and monitor someone else. Other times, there are no internal resources to download assignments to.

As a result, the following trends can be seen in many small companies:

- Owners are stressed and overworked, while staff are underutilized and under capacity.
- Staff members are not given an

opportunity to grow and develop in their roles, and may perceive a lack of trust or confidence in their ability. The company loses good people.

• Owners are always in a reactive state, putting out fires in their business daily, instead of a visionary or proactive state.

• Delegation happens at the very last minute, and staff has little understanding of either the overall project or expectations for the task.

The easiest way to fix this problem is before it starts. Create a solid team of staff members around you who are well-trained and prepared to support the business. Attract and retain qualified and quality people who can be cross-trained and promoted within the company. Ensure that communication flows throughout the business, so that everyone has the product and service knowledge to step in and assist when necessary.

4. Learn to Say "No"

It's easy to fall into the habit of saying yes to

everything. You are, after all, the business owner, right? No one can complete these tasks as well as you? You'll lose that customer if you don't help them with their garage sale, right?

Wrong. The most successful business owners have a keen understanding of how their time is best spent, and delegate the remaining responsibilities to trusted others. It's too easy to say yes to every request in the moment, and later feel overwhelmed when it's added to your to do list. You may not ruffle any feathers, but what toll does it take on your stress level? Your workload? Your time is valuable – so protect it!

Remember that if it is too challenging to say no immediately, you can always request some time to think about it. This way, you can evaluate your workload and realistically decide whether or not you can take on a new project. Then, stand by your decision, or assist in bringing in the necessary resources to get it done.

5. Create (and keep!) a Strict Schedule

While multi-tasking is a desirable skill, it is often a time thief. Attempting to do too many things at one time ensures that nothing gets done. As a business owner, you need to be able to focus and concentrate on essential projects without interruptions.

The only way to do this is the commit to a strict schedule. Once you understand your work style and concentration patterns, you can allocate periods of the day to specific tasks. This includes personal and leisure time. Schedule it, and stick to it.

Make sure that you schedule time for: list-creation and prioritization, email messages, telephone messages, internal meetings, client meetings, meeting preparation, "me-time", family time, recreation and fitness, daily business tasks, and blocks for focused work.

Remember that there is a training period involved in beginning a new routine – for yourself and those around you. Use your voicemail, out-of-office email message, and a closed door to begin to let people know when you will not be disturbed.

6. Make Decisions

The choice to not make a decision is a decision in itself. The most successful business owners have the ability to make good decisions quickly and efficiently, and do not waste time deliberating over simple choices.

In leadership positions, often people are afraid of making the wrong decision or looking foolish if they make a mistake in front of staff. What they don't realize is that hesitating or avoiding decision making actually impacts their leadership just as much, or more, than making the wrong decision. Not only can being indecisive be personally stressful, but it is also stressful for those around you whose tasks are waiting on your choices.

Remember, you must make the best decision with the information you have, in the time frame you have to make it. No one expects you to be a fortune teller – be decisive, make some mistakes, and learn from them.

7. Manage Telephone Interruptions

This is a huge source of time theft that can easily be managed and avoided. If you are available to take phone calls at any time of day, you are setting yourself up to take work home in the evenings. The phone will always ring when you are focused on an important task, and this is something that can easily be avoided.

Figure out when you are most productive. Is it in the morning or the afternoon? Before, during, or after lunch? Once you have identified this time period, set your phone on "do not disturb" or have your calls directed to voicemail. If you do not have a receptionist, a variety of automatic answering systems are available for a nominal fee. To structure your phone time further, let callers know on your voicemail what specific time of day is best to reach you via phone. Then, set that time aside to receive and return phone calls.

8. Keep Your Work Environment Organized

Have you ever tried to make dinner in a messy kitchen? More of your time is spent looking for and cleaning dishes and tools than actually spent cooking the meal.

The same goes for your work environment. If your desk and office is in a constant state of chaos, then your mind will be too. In fact, some studies have revealed that the average business leader spends nearly four weeks each year navigating through messy or cluttered desks, looking for lost information. Does that sound like productive time to you?

Once you make the initial clean sweep, it's easy to maintain order in the chaos:

- Tidy your desk at the beginning and end of each day. Attach pertinent documents to your to do list, or have clear and organized folders for loose papers.
- Organize your supplies drawer so you have easy access to tools like pens, post-it notes, staplers and highlighters. Every

minute counts!

• Only have the documents and files on which you are currently working on your desk. The rest should be neatly filed on a side table for later retrieval.

• Keep personal items (like photos or memorabilia) out of your primary line of vision. These can be distracting and encourage daydreaming.

As for your office or store, there are many ways to make its layout more conducive to effective time management.
Try:

• Minimizing the distance between the reception desk and electronics like photocopies and fax machines.

• Keep a clear line of sight between your office and the most productive area of your business, so you are aware of what is happening amongst your staff.

• Organize shelves and filing cabinets so files are not only easily accessed, but out of sight when not being used. Consider putting sliding doors or cabinets in storage areas, and remember that the floor is not a storage cabinet.

9. Keep Your Filing System Organized

If your data isn't organized properly, you will waste hundreds of hours searching for the documents you need on a regular basis. This includes both electronic and hard copy files. They all need to be organized and up to date.

Customer databases and enquiry records are worth their weight in gold. You can't afford to get behind when updating this information, or poorly store it for later retrieval. There are many easy to use software programs that will manage and organize customer databases for you. This act doesn't need to be a time consuming or tedious exercise.

A simple way to manage information is to keep it in short, medium, and long term files for both hard and electronic copies. Create shortcuts on your desktop for folders or files you constantly access. Have short-term files available on your desk, medium-term files available within an arm's reach, and long-term files stored in cabinets.

10. Clearly Communicate – Never Assume

One of the biggest issues for time management in business – and likely the world – is miscommunication. This is a dangerous issue that can cripple any business, including yours. Establishing and enforcing clear policies on things like accurate note taking, task assignments, and phone messages will ensure that your staff understand the importance of clear and accurate communication.

The easiest habit to start to curb miscommunication is simple: write everything down. Carry a notepad and jot down key points, figures, agreements and deadlines. Don't assume you'll remember later – you have at least a hundred other things to remember.

Some other simple strategies are:

- Return all communication promptly, including email, letters, faxes and phone calls
- Repeat back phone messages, phone numbers and other figures to confirm you recorded the information correctly.
- Record appointments in your agenda the moment you make them. Otherwise, you'll likely forget.
- Double check and confirm everything – addresses, phone numbers, meeting locations and times.
- Maintain accurate and up to date customer contact logs with dates, times, and phone numbers.
- Post checklists in your store or office for routine operations procedures.
- Announce any changes to the policies and procedures manual immediately.

11. Stop Duplicating Efforts

This is a key element of time management that is closely related to effective communication. Studies have continually shown that many businesses often duplicate and triplicate efforts that need only be completed once.

When you have clear systems and procedures in place, your staff will not need to reinvent the wheel each time the task needs to be completed. Meeting minutes and individual task assignments will ensure everyone is on the same page and understands their personal responsibilities.

One simple example of this includes re-reading your to-do list each hour to determine what the next important item is. If your list is already structured by priority, this is a needless task. If two staff members are working on similar projects, but unaware of the other, the work will not only be inconsistent, but the efforts will be duplicated. These are easy problems to fix, once they have been identified and communicated.

12. Say Goodbye to Procrastination and Perfectionism

Procrastination is something we all face at one

time or another – and likely have since our school days. However, given the pace that the world operates at today, you will only fall behind your competitor if you allow procrastination to rule your day. So how you do avoid it? It's simple. Stop, and just get started, no matter how boring, tedious, or painful the project may be. Reward yourself by crossing each step off your to-do list.

Many small business owners also fall victim to perfectionism, which can be paralyzing. The fear that there isn't enough time or resources to get it 'perfect' will sometimes stop you dead in your tracks. Perfectionism can also hinder your ability to delegate and say no to tasks you believe no one else can complete better. Do the best you can with the time and resources you have – and just get started.

13. Plan Your Work, Work Your Plan

Have you ever placed an advertisement on the fly because it was "cheaper", "faster", or "more urgent" than creating a marketing plan? Do you and your staff have a clear idea of where your business is headed over the next six to 12 months, or even five years?

Many studies show that less than 10% of small businesses have up to date marketing and business plans, as compared to the majority of large corporations and public companies, which have both.

Marketing and business plans take time and effort to create – but they work, and pay off in a big way. They also save you time and money as compared to a haphazard or fly-by-the-seat-of-your-pants strategy. With a marketing plan in place, you will have an idea of how many ads you will be placing in a year, which will earn you a volume discount. Your marketing materials will complement each other, and deliver the same message to the same target audience. Designers will charge less for a package of collateral than for individual collateral items.

A business plan will provide you with a guide to reference when making decisions. You can repeatedly ask if the endeavor at hand will contribute to your overall vision, or just seems like a good idea or price.

Remember that planning includes both short and long-term time frames, and applies to both your daily to-do list and your marketing budget. It provides you with the means to measure your progress, assists in identifying priorities, and helps to manage your time.

14. Avoid Needless Meetings

This may seem like a time theft issue that is out of your control, but it's not. You are in control of your own time, and through strict scheduling can establish a structure for internal and external meetings that everyone around you can work within.

Minimize impromptu internal meetings by letting your staff know when you're available for a 'quick chat' and when you are not. If it is important, ask them to schedule a time to meet with you that works with both of your schedules. This not only saves you time, but encourages staff to find solutions to their own issues, and only approach you with more urgent or challenging matters.

You can't avoid having meetings altogether, but you can avoid having unstructured ones. Ask for, or create an agenda for each meeting you attend, with a clear objective and an amount of time allocated to each item. This will keep your meetings focused and on task. If a meeting does run late, give yourself a reasonable buffer, and politely leave for your next appointment. You can always follow up with a colleague to catch-up on the pertinent items you may have missed.

15. Establish Clear Policies and Procedures

A clear policy and procedures manual is like a marketing or business plan – it takes time to create, but ultimately saves everyone in your company time, money and effort. A step-by-step guide to "the way we do things here" is an invaluable resource for your existing and new staff, and provides clear expectations for how you like things done.
Too many businesses make up policies and

procedures on the fly – creating dangerous scenarios where mistakes are made and expectations are not clear. Some items that should be included in a comprehensive policy and procedures manual include:

- Recruitment
- Customer relations
- Customer enquiries
- Customer complaints
- Returns
- Exchanges
- Late Payments
- Salary structure
- Bonus structure
- Employee review
- Theft
- Harassment

16. Keep the Right Set of Tools

The equipment your business needs to operate and grow effectively should always be on hand, or easily contracted out. This is specific to each company, and closely related to costs – including the cost of your time.

Whether you are a high-tech business or a local retailer, knowledge of the latest advancements in technology will increase your efficiency. It will help you stay on top of the competitor, maintain your position as an expert, and perhaps provide an easier way of getting things done.

Always ask yourself if these purchases are essential to your business. Could you perhaps make these purchases from a second hand dealer to minimize cost? Is it more cost effective to outsource or sub-contract the tasks to someone with access to this equipment, or to buy the equipment yourself?

If your business relies on tools and technology for daily tasks (such as the trades profession), then obtaining the best quality you can afford is crucial.

17. Maintain Your Equipment

This may seem obvious, but you'll understand the vitality of this if your network server has ever crashed, or point of sale system has malfunctioned. Your business can be slowed to a stand-still if your equipment is not in good working order. Of course there are always instances that can't be predicted, but regular maintenance of your essential equipment will reduce these occurrences and help to anticipate when old equipment needs to be repaired or replaced.

Personal Time Management Strategy

Choose the top five tips from this chapter that you think will help you the most, given your personal time management research. Write them down, with three corresponding actions that you will start tomorrow. For example, if you are going to set a strict schedule, three actions might be to establish the schedule, communicate it to your staff, and re-record your voicemail message.

So What Do You Do From Here?

Take Action! If you're already an accomplished business owner, use this book as direction to enhance the speed of your business success. If you are not as successful and accomplished as you would like to be, then the smartest things to do are:

A. Learn To Earn

B. Invest In Professional Help to Drive the Speed of Your Business Success

C. Be an Action Taker

Concentrate on strategies to Learn and the Earn will follow! If you are serious about taking the next step, then go to work on yourself, study other business successes, understand small business marketing strategies, and become a sponge for new (proven) material. The amazing thing about the game of business is that when you put proven processes to work, and continue to follow them, an abundance of success will follow. The biggest mistake is to start a process and then subsequently fallback into your old habits after a short time.

Above all, get the knowledge you need to be in the game of business. Would you bet your money and challenge Tiger Woods to a game of golf if you knew nothing about golf and had never played golf before? Of course not! However, it is amazing to me how many new small business people start the game of business against seasoned professionals without first developing the necessary knowledge to be successful. Then, they fail and blame the market, the economy, their location, etc. In fact, I made this very same mistake years ago. It will cost you more time and money than you want to lose and you will have more grief and stress than you bargained for.

If you have a business and have not yet managed to start to create wealth and systems that allow you to take time off, build retirement accounts, or pay for your children's college, then learn and master the keys outlined in my book. I am a huge advocate of education and mentorships. Get the right information, find someone that knows how to walk you through them, and watch your quality of life take new shape or contact me.

For all my best tips, tricks, marketing resources, training or help, make sure you visit

my website at www.anncardencoaching.com
or contact me today at
ann@anncardencoaching.com

ABOUT THE AUTHOR

Ann Carden is the wife of Clayton for 34 years, a mother of Shane and Shay and mother-in-law to Callie. She is a Christian women with a strong faith in Jesus Christ as her Lord and Savior. She believes that we all have a calling to make a difference in the world and we are not just on this earth to exist and live for ourselves. She is a believer that gifts and talents should be shared to better one another's lives. Ann is passionate about consistent learning and is dedicated to teaching others. She has a strong belief that everyone in our great country, the United States Of America, has the opportunity to succeed. It is their personal choice to grow and become all they can be, or settle for their circumstances. Her personal determination, passion and strength comes from her faith in Christ, her family and friends.

As a coach to others in business, she is dedicated to help them build their dreams and enjoy what they do.

For more about Ann's professional background, services or to contact Ann, visit www.anncardencoaching.com

May God Bless You Abundantly!